LEARNING INFLUENCING PERFORMANCE

FACTORS

JOHN LOK

2020 MAR Published

Contents

Preface

Introduction

This book is concerned how to apply behavioral psychology method to predict labor psychology and solve labor argument challenges in societies. Research question: How to raise labor productivity?

This book is one teaching book to give some behavioral economy concepts to indicate why labor will act to do this behaviors in societies. Theories include: online knowledgeable concept, globalization job concept , useful indicator concept, standard growth enhancing policy, standard growth enhancing policy, outsourcing, national environment policy, tax policy.

The first part, I shall explain what the labour economy concept is. I shall indicate evidences to give my reasons to predict knowledgeable jobs, such as online office workers, online freelance electronic book authors, online survey researcher, online business researcher etc. internet channel office jobs which will be caused popularly in the future. So, I shall indicate why employers need to concern this online job issue because nowadays employees prefer to work free time and no overtime often.

Then, I shall indicate why employers need to concern labor ethic issue and how it can improve the absolute living standard to reduce poor occurrence. I shall indicate some developed countries, e.g. America, England etc. countries and some developing countries, e.g. China and Hong Kong. To give reasons to indicate why this countries‘ economy growth can not improve the low income level householders living standard in fact. Moreover, I also indicate one economy method to recommend how governments can use this policy to attempt to improve the low income level householder living of standard more accurately to assist employers to raise productivity indirectly.

Finally, I shall explain why employers ought to consider the ethics to labor to judge whether how to do right decisions to keep the fairness productivity and the welfare and benefits to whose employees. I also indicate why labor ethics and productivity and even economic growth which has close relationship, so why economists and employers who need to concern ethics to labor to judge to make any social benefits of decisions. Finally, I shall give economic concepts and assumptions to let readers to judge how to do connect moral behavior when to decide labor welfare and raising productivity. It is suitable to any economists or employers who have need to learn how to do the right behavior to satisfy whose employees' emotion to raise productivity. How behavioral economics can provide more realistic psychological foundations. This book is intended to provide an introduction to the approach and methods of behavioral economics, and to some of its major findings, application, and promising new directions. I shall explain how the process of behavior economic field develops, then I shall show what methods are used to measure behavioral economy. Next, I shall indicate what the main two categories of behavioral economy are as well as I shall explain what risky and uncertain outcomes of individual behavior economic theories are as well as what behavioral game theory is. Finally, I shall explain behavioral economic principles of policy makers or decision makers as well as I shall also analyze whether behavioral economy and psychology which has close relationship. This book is suitable to any economists or policy makers or individual consumption makers or students or working people who have interest learn how to apply behavioral economy to judge to do the most reasonable or the most right economic activities in everyday life. The end, I shall apply above mentions to explain what the differences are between labor economy and behavioral economy clearly. This book is suitable to any students, labor or behavioral economists, employers and employees to read. I also hope you can learn more new and unique economic knowledge to assist your economic research in the future.

I shall explain what the concept is that behavioral economics can provide more realistic psychological foundations. This book is intended to provide an introduction to the approach and methods of behavioral economics, and to some of its major findings, application, and promising new directions.

In second part, it shall indicate how the process of behaviour economic field develops, then I shall show what methods are used to measure behavioural economy. Next, I shall indicate what the main two categories of behavioural economy are as well as I shall explain what risky and uncertain outcomes of individual behavior economic theories are as well as what behavioral game theory is. Finally, I shall explain behavioral economic principles of policy makers or decision makers as well as I shall also analyze whether behavioral economy and psychology which has close relationship. This book is suitable to any economists or policy makers or individual consumption makers or students or working people who have interest learn how to apply behavioural economy to judge to do the most reasonable or the most right economic activities in everyday life.

In third part, I shall let reader can learn how to use policy to solve economic challenges. I shall analyse the processes from this aspects. Such as, human development policy, tax policy, educational development policy, national environment protection policy, regulatory management policy, private investment encouragement policy, behavioral economy and psychology leadership policy. I also indicate example and cases to explain why these policies can be applied to assist economic growth to any countries for long term.

This book is suitable to any economists or policy makers or individual consumption makers or students or businessmen who have interest to learn how to apply behavioural economy methods to judge to do the most reasonable or the most right economic activities to achieve economic benefit in everyday life. In my this book, the main important aim, I give examples to explain how to apply psychological and behavioral economic both view point related methods to raise labor

Prologue

BRIEF CONTENTS

Bibliography

CHAPTER ONE

KNOWLEDGEABLE JOBS

Why does online knowledgeable jobs (HOME DEMOTE WORK) will be raised productivity ?

In what way has globalization affected employers choose online work to provide to local or overseas to raise productivity? Is online work still a useful working place environment for local and overseas employers to raise productivity in a globalized online age, such as online electronic books' authors, online office administration or online surveys or online researchers etc. kind of online jobs supplying? Our age is entering an online business environment, such as online electronic air tickets sale, online electronic books publishing, online advertising and online shopping and website design service promotion , online university education etc. different kind of online businesses from internet. It seems online channel can increase global online job chances to affect that our live and our job nature to be changed every day. For example, online electronic book publishing business will be popular, many different countries' readers who like to buy electronic books to study, due to these online electronic book shops, e.g. Amazon, lulu, book Rix, book tango etc. electronic book stores which can provide free charge to deliver cheaper paper books to any overseas countries' readers' homes and which paper book prices are more cheaper to compare to book shops' paper books process after who have paid to buy any electronic books or paper books from these online book stores websites. Moreover, these readers can read these book stores' electronic books from online publishing sellers' websites to download these electronic books to study at homes or any libraries etc. computer provision of places easily and conveniently. So readers do not need to walk to any book shops to buy any paper books and who also do not need to bring any heavy paper books back to homes conveniently. Hence, electronic publishers can provide electronic book authors' job chances to write their books and type to computers to register to be online authors to publish whose electronic or paper books to earn loyalty income at home very easily. Also, the globalizing online job nature can change the customized office work style. It won't need staffs go to office to work from 9:00 AM to 6:00 PM. In general office workers need to spend eight to ten working hours with five or six working days within per week commonly. Hence, online office workers don't need to pay transportation fee and lunch cost, due who can work at their home when who turn on their computer to enter whose employers' websites to work and make email communication to connect between them conveniently. So, I feel the online electronic book authors and online office administration jobs which will be popular further occupations to be provided from global online job structure style and many labors will like to work online, then who can raise productivity conveniently when who work at home in the future. Beside, due to online (internet) is very popular and cheap cost to be needed to spend expenditure from employer. So, internet will build the relationships between workplaces and every staff role identity and everyday life and online working environments can connect them to work in the process of globalization in the future. Also, our everyday life and work is entering in a globalizing world. It emphasizes on time and space compression and the importance of virtual space and experience in our daily lives of many people, the working style seems spent online working time to change how our social traditional work roles and our traditional office working places-based environments to home online working environments further long time in the future. So, employers ought plan to prepare online working methods to let their employees to raise productivity.

Why does knowledgeable online jobs will raise economic growth?

Social science can explain knowledgeable jobs will be useful and popular and assisting labors to raise productivity to work at home online working environments. Within social science, in such discipline is sociology and human psychology and geography which indicates internet technology have changed to online working place environment, sense of working place, online employee role identity, everyday online work and life style, website global working communication and email online communication working interconnections. It seems internet brings access to social, economic and political resources to effect change to both individual and social working conditions, such as employers accept to attempt to use internet to assist office staffs to work at home, e.g. many book publishing businesses like to attempt to publish electronic books from online book store, instead of book shops channel to sell paper books. So these online book stores give chance to authors to publish electronic books or online paper books from online sale channel to earn loyalty income. For example, Amazon online electronic bookstore can publish electronic books and online paper books to sell all one day 24 hours to any countries' readers from its website, so when any countries' readers can enter its website to choose any different kind of subjects of electronic books to buy by visa card conveniently. Such as fiction, psychology, economy, science, law, architecture, medicine, commerce, management etc. subjects. So, any country's reader who does not need to buy air tickets to go to the country's book shop to buy the paper book, who only needs to pay visa card to buy the electronic or online paper books from Amazon publishing's website to buy any countries' electronic and paper books and then the overseas reader can choose either to download it from whose home computer or pays more price to deliver the online paper book to post to whose country conveniently. Hence, this online bookstore sale method will be popular and many free work authors will choose to work to raise the productivity of more quality electronic books numbers from this internet channel.

However, the consequences of global change are far from uniform with globalizing influences and adapted as new technological, economic and online working cultural experiences are incorporated by any countries' staffs of any cities, towns and rural areas into their everyday work lives from long distance easily. Since one company can employ different countries' staffs to work from internet working channel at their homes. For example, a America company can employ overseas countries' staffs to work at the same time together by sending job duties from email communication channel among them when the America company has any job arrangement to notify to any staff to finish it any time, then the overseas staff finish the job and who can send whose finished documents to whose America employer any time. It seems the overseas staffs whose working hours can be flexible and those working hours have no regular office working hours to be fixed time table, so they do not need to work in any fixed working time table every working days, who can send their finished office documents to whose employers after who have finished their documents by either email communication channel or office online website downloads office download any time conveniently.

It will be a new working style position that online working globalization is in a new stage. We are living in an age of very rapid and fluid flow of information, ideas, products and people which are having an effect of a variety of scales. I shall indicate evidences to explain why employers will encounter online knowledgeable jobs to raise productivity in a globalizing world by sociology concept. I shall focus on research into the connections between our everyday online life style, online working place and online working role identity. The first is that everyday online life is the manifestation of social existence and always involves either distant or direct interaction with other people. Such as we can use internet email channel to communicate with overseas friends or strange people, even employers or employees can also use email to exchange to receive and send their office documents by email or company website any time conveniently. Good example includes such things are as online participation in work, employment, cultural events, and recreation, shopping and communication from internet channel. It is related to employees are working in whose home working places and their home working place are possible to connect their overseas employers' offices and however, readily these may be separated in far distant conceptual terms, such as an online working environment. The employee's home is such whose employer's office, who can work at home from online channel conveniently. When who receives whose employer's email about what job duties who needs to do every day. Then, who sees his employer's email, then either if who did not understand how to do whose job duties clearly, who can send email back to ask whose employers to explain how who needs to do whose office job duties by email communication channel again easily. Even after who finish whose office job duties on that day or another day, then who can send finished office job duties to whose employers by email conveniently. In this view, online working places and sense of online working places are produced by different countries' large enterprise employers and overseas employees interacting together. At the same time, employees and employers whose sense are contacted by employees' individual role identity from email or office website communication channel any time. Thus, traditional office working environment is constrained and enabled by different countries' working histories and cultures and social class backgrounds and economic conditions and job opportunities, working positions of power and working geographical locations and development of local change and distant social interaction. In the future, online working place will be changed from traditional socially significant to online social relationship; underlying this sense of online working place will be the notion that some employers and employees themselves ought feel that life. Moreover, online working place is the possibility of non controlling employees' working time, due to working hours are flexible and employers' working places sizes are very limited to supply to many staffs to work in a limited office working place in the same working time. It seems online home environment will be very popular, due to every employee will use whose home to work to finish whose office documents at home every day any time very conveniently as well as employers won't need to spend much expenditure to pay for large sizes of office rent when the employer needs to rent more than one room office at more than one floor in one building. Hence, company's website expenditure can reduce the employers' office rent seriously. Moreover, employees can be dominated by feelings towards changing general office working place to online working at home as well as changing fixed working time table to flexible working time table, e.g. the staff can see whose employer's email to know what office job duties who needs to do tonight, so who will finish whose office documents and will send whose finished office documents to whose employer by email tomorrow. So, home online working environment is seen as an ideal home working place, and home online working environment which is quiet, safe and it has certain valued facilities and home online working environment is such as the type of residents in the employee's living building. This sense of living and online work place will be held by residents who will be employed in professional/ managerial/ technical etc. occupations. Hence, local employees won't catch any transportation to go to office as well as overseas employees won't also catch planes to go to whose employer's country's office to work, due to who can use online email communication or office website communication channels to work together conveniently. However, working facilities will be one online computer working commodity which is purchasable, useable and exchangeable and saleable to any employees are located at home and employers are located at office, and after a flexible working time table is discarded easily by employer, due to whose website or office email can receive any employee's individual finished office documents by every employee's individual email communication any time very conveniently. Moreover, home online working place is also like a stage on every employee's life is lived out. The employee will feel that whose life and working time is lived at home together at the same time. Similar to feel commodity sense of home and the working place which are the same location, but it is distinguished from it by the establishment of arriving strange and far distant of the employee's local or overseas employer's office when the employee's working place is family interacting to the employee's house or home.

Our world is entering globalization, people are connecting in an increasing number of ways. It is clear also that is the face of globalization, the ways of our everyday working life is either constituted which are still shaped by local expenditure of working place or is by where the firm's overseas employees love locally, regionally and nationally or is by the access who have limited to office resources and home office online working locations opportunity changing from general office working environment to home online working environment. Roberston (1992) shows is that" this is not just about economic processes, but about social and cultural issues are as well. In the early part of the 21 ST century, it is necessary to see this as a set of processes that encompass economic, political, social, cultural and environmental changes."

Why employers need to considerate the low
income level worker whose living of standard challenge.

Is globalization influenced to new online knowledgeable jobs to be provided to raise low income level worker's living od standard? One of the key areas of debate among theorists is the extent to which globalization is a new phenomenon or stage in a process. When it began and the path that it has followed and thus how new it is. Such as internet is used in communication aspect in early, e.g. hospital or war email communication channel. Then, many businessmen discovered online electronic commerce is also one online sale and purchase method. So, it will cause online office workers or online freelance online jobs, e.g. electronic book authors working style or electronic book reading cultural existed in our society in common possibly in the future. However, I recognize globalization is a misleading concept since what is described as globalization has been happening for the 500 years history ago. Rather what is new is that human are entering an age of transition, such as online knowledgeable workers or knowledgeable nature of different jobs will be caused from online working environment popularly. There are key processes of globalization: the economic, often is seen as the central process, the political, social, cultural and online working environment. Every natural economy needs to maintain the rate of growth, employment, welfare provision and minimum wage balance levels, so it will cause knowledgeable jobs provided, such as online organized labors, it also will change the traditional office organizational environment to cause online new organizational home work environment popularly in the future. Hence, economic and political has close connection, political and cultural has also close connection, cultural and social has also close connection, social and working environment has also connection. After all these connections cause globalization finally, then the new online knowledgeable working environment, such as online jobs will be required by global office employees popularly in the future. It will bring many online workers supply to the employment market in the future. As capital in the new globalized economy has a limited attachment to working place, production centers, such as offices, factories or farms which locate any where it is competitively advantages to do so, and economic activity moves to where labor is cheapest or raw materials is the least expensive. It can be raised demand to online knowledgeable workers demand in global competitive employment environment directly. For example, cultural, social, global expansion of Mc Donald's and other fast food chains will be entered to the online sale channel. Hence, environmental globalization raises human awareness, includes a new view of the natural and the social worlds to environmental protection message. These message source is from online channel popularly nowadays. Online organizing environment and living will influence our everyday working worlds. Due to many industrial cities and life will be not needed by global employers. However, industrial cities concentrate on demanding in developing countries, e.g. China, India, Korea etc. countries. So, developed countries, such as America, England, Japan etc. countries' employers will need many online knowledgeable employees to help them to work from online work place environment popular in the future. Later, knowledgeable online working environment will be popular to developing countries when which economy had developed mature in the future. So, it is possible online jobs will raise low income level householders' living of standard.

CHAPTER TWO

LIVING STANDARD IMPROVEMENT

Is income a useful indicator to measure living standard to assist economic growth?

Nowadays, developing countries, such as India, China, Hong Kong, etc. and developed countries, such as America, England etc. which are facing social challenges. For example, many low income level householders whose income level can't be raised and inflation is also high in society. Although, these developing countries' economy is growing, but which can not raise the low income level householders' income level to let them have afford to buy one house in minimum in whose country, even these low income level family have no enough income to buy foods to eat and cloths to wear easily. Also, the developed countries' economy had arrived the mature growing stage, but which also can not give any benefits to whose low level income level income householders group. Hence, governments have responsibilities to find methods to solve these challenges, such as: How to reduce poor occurrence? How much does economic growth help the poor? How can social policy help? Can a country have a sizeable low-wage sector of house to provide to the poor? What role can public service social spending better for the poor?

Justice is the distribution of income and wealth is fairest. Any country's government needs play a large role in determining it's citizen's abilities to do common occupation, what job choices are preferences to them, how to raise employment of motivation and what social circumstances are to cause households have no poor occurrence to cause many low level income jobs to do to earn income in society. In order to reduce the unfair income distribution between rich and poor people. Why it is important to improve unfair income treatment between rich and poor people to any countries? However, in a rich and growing economic country, such as America, England etc. , which are difficult to justify stagnant living standards for those at the floor bottom low income people nowadays. Although, these developed countries' economy are growing, but which can not give benefits to this low level income households group. However, I suggest any country ought favor not simply a satisfactory level of living standards for the poor people, but it ought consider how to improve or review poor people living standards every year. Analysts typically set the poverty line at 50 or 60 percent of the median income within each country. In general, poverty means to level of resources insufficient to achieve a minimal acceptable standard of living as well as people tends to experience poverty as relative is to living standards by comparison in any country's citizen's own society. If the absolute incomes or living standards for the poor grow less rapidly than those of households in the middle income level in the country. So, it seems that it is not fair economic growth in these developing countries..

How to apply " standard growth enhancing policy" to improve low income level householders living of standard to raise productivity

Is income a useful indicator of living standards? Income is a resource that allows any country's households to acquire the sort of things e.g. food, housing, medical care, transportation, education, entertainment etc. needs. So, which are needed for a minimal decent standard of living. Income also is comparatively easy to measure. However, causing poor factors might have many reasons, such as illness, temporary unemployment, a large amount of bonus reduction, overtime long time working hours, family members unemployment, even economic decline (falling down), so these factors can reduce jobs supply to any countries to cause poor occurrence. However, any countries‘ income measures seldom include the value of government service and in kind benefit, such as pension, unemployment assistance etc. as well as some low income households have assets (savings in bank, and owned home). So, it seems income is not an accurate measure to the actual living standard to the low income people numbers in the countries effectively. If income is not an accurate measure to actual living standard, then it can not improve the low income level householders of living standard and productivity level will be reduced because these low income level labors can not get reasonable salaries and unfair welfare to work from whose employers. Otherwise, the high income level labors can get increased salaries and fair welfare to work from whose employers.

When these both low and high income level labors work in same company, the low income level labors will feel angry to work unhappy, then it is possible that who will decrease their productivity.

The poor people numbers will be reduced possibly. How to evaluate the actual poor people numbers decreasing? In think when the degree to the country which economic growth boosts the income level of low and households to rise their general savings amounts to the income level of middle households. Then, the country's poor people numbers will be decreasing, due to this group of the numbers of incomes level of low households has been decreasing and it's numbers has been increasing to the income level of middle group, then productivity will also raise to every employers in any country.

In general, economic growth is assumed that poor households get more jobs, work more hours and/or receives higher wages. Hence, when one country measure economic growth, which can apply the relationship between per capita GDP and low income households of numbers between the past year and current year to measure the rising or falling numbers per capita GDP in the low and income households group, for example, in Sweden, Denmark, Norway, the Netherlands and Finland countries which net transfers are received by low income level households increased significantly between 1979 year and 2007 year. But, average earnings, were flat in Demarks country, when in Sweden and Finland countries which declined sharply during those countries' deep recessions in the early 1990 year. Otherwise, in the United Kingdom, the period was from 1979 year to 1995 year, it saw no changes in transfers pension or retirement savings from

United Kingdom government and a slight drop in earnings, but from 1999 year to 2005 year, social earning increased slightly, but more important was a large rise in net government pension and retirement saving transfers, which resulted in a sizeable increase in low income level incomes group. When net government pension or retirement savings transfers to citizen increased this was caused by economic growth. In general, economic growth allows policy makers to boost inflation-adjusted benefit levels for pension or retirement saving transfer to citizen programs, which will increased the incomes of pension or retirement saving benefit recipients. With GDP rising, government social benefit pension or retirement saving transfers as a share of GDP tended to remark more or less constant.

However, in some countries, the rise in pension of retirement saving net transfers was achieved in part by reduction of income or profit taxes for low income households or low business profit households, since the 1970 year, most of the world's rich nations, such as America, united Kingdom have not significantly increased the share of their GDP that goes to pensions or retirement savings transfer for the low income level poor households. It seems that if any country hoped the low income level of householders numbers will be increase, which ought need to upgrade their low income level to go up middle income level in society, then its economic growth will be raising. How economic growth can boost incomes for the poor households. It seems economic growth has made rising low income level of households is more likely, but several countries are exceptions. They experienced growing per capita GDP, but little or no improvement in the income of low income level of households, such as Hong Kong has seven million people who are living in a small city. Although, it was encountering economic growth from 1970 year in beginning, but the low income level of households had little or no improvement, it was possible that the numbers of Hong Kong low income level of households are more than the middle or high income level of households seriously. So, the HK economic growth seems not improve low income level of households to assist this low income level of households to raise whose income to be risen to the middle income level of households group. The reason is possible that the failure of some governments to increase public transfers as the economy grows is a key part of reason. But why did not more economic growth reach the low income level of poor households in the form of rising market income? For example, in HK, whether economic growth is likely to directly benefit the poor group's employment hours reduction and rising hourly wage levels. However, I discovered that HK economic growth produced no increase in the wage or salary market rate of low level of income households and without employment hours reduction and without rising hourly wage levels. So, HK economic growth seems to raise more job supply in the employment market, but it seems without employment hours reduction. Otherwise, it's economic growth rises employment hours, but without rising hourly wage. Hence, it seems low income level householders of numbers and economic growth have close relationship to any country, so employers need to concern their labors numbers of low income level to raise their income to be middle income level in society.

CHAPTER THREE

LABOR ETHIC

I recommend this economic policy to reduce poor occurrence, such as growth on average benefit the poor as much as anyone lives in the country's society, such as "standard growth enhancing policy" should be at the center of any poverty reduction strategy. I believe economic growth is the most powerful instrument for reducing poverty, due to many businessmen have enough money to invest to their countries to do any kind of businesses, then the jobs supply will be raised any many people can get any jobs supply number is more than job seekers number, then it is no doubt, the unemployment numbers will be reduced. When many people have new jobs to do and who can earn enough wages to prepare to save more money in bank.

What has been the impact of economic growth on employment hours and wages? In fact, work hours are matter a great deal for the incomes of poor group of households in developed countries, such as United States or United Kingdom or developing countries, such as Hong Kong, China etc. countries. For example, HK economic growth has a large influence to raise employment hours more than rising wage levels, such as HK general working hours are risen up to 10 to 12 hours or more per week working days to low income level of households, but the low income level of households group has not been rising wage level generally. So, I feel HK economic growth could not give any benefits to the low income level of households, such as without reduction employment hours and without raising wage level to the low income level of households in HK. Also, HK's economic growth only raises many jobs supply in HK society. Otherwise, America economic growth can give benefits to low income level of households, such as reduction employment hours, rising wage level to low income level of households and raising jobs supply in America society. Hence, the developed countries, such as America , England which economic growth can give more benefits to low income level of households. Otherwise, the developing countries, such as India, China, Korea which economic growth can not give more benefits to the low income level of households and these developing countries will cause disadvantages to this low income level of poor group in society. It is possible that the developing countries' low income level of households often need to increase to spend more working hours to assist whose employers to develop whose employers' business, due to their employers do not want to increase to employ extra workers or staffs to assist whose business development, who need whose current employees to raise more extra working hours to work to raise work efficiency when these developing countries are encountering the economic growth stage.

For example, HK employers do not concern moral issues about abnormal working hours influence. The outcome is either Hong Kong labors work long time working hours abnormally who can not rise Hong Kong economic growth or who can rise Hong Kong economic growth in long time. Generally, Hong Kong employers choose to pay less salary expenditure to need many extra labors to work abnormal working hours to help them to rise productivity, but who don't concern that long time working factor will influence unhealthy to current workers due to who need to work long time working hours abnormally in long time and it seems to cause their workers will reduce productivity and inefficiency in long time.

Although, it is possible that HK labors can be increased extra abnormal working hours to work to rise Hong Kong employers' productivity and assist HK social economy will be grown up in short term, but it is also possible that it can't rise Hong Kong economic growth due to their unhealthy or sick increasing to cause productivity declining and inefficiency in long time. Thus, I shall find evidence to analyze whether Hong Kong labors need to work abnormal long time working hours. Otherwise, who will decline Hong Kong economic growth and reduce productivity and inefficiency in long time as well as I shall give suggestion to indicate whether either current workers work abnormal long time working hours or employers ought choose to employ more extra part time workers to assist current labors to rise their productivity to decide which is the best choice to raise HK economic growth and efficient productivity in long time.

Effects on Hong Kong employment of working time reduction is found to be difficult to predict. The results of Hong Kong macroeconomic simulations of the effects on employments of working time reduction rely heavily on certain basic assumptions, such as how many hours people will actually work or how productivity and pay levels will develop. Whether HK abnormal working hours will assist

HK social economic growth or economic falling down in long term.

The reasons cause Hong Kong labors who need to work abnormal long time working hours. In fact, it isn't the reason that the Hong Kong high skillful labors market is shortage to supply for the nature of some occupations, e.g. hospital doctors and nurses, university teachers, law firm lawyers etc. professional occupations. HK has many high qualification university students graduation, it has enough labor supply to high labor market every year. The reason is that employers don't like to spend more salary to increase to employ extra labors to share current workers workload, such as low skillful and hardworking labors, such as cleaners, securities, waiters and high skillful professionals, such as hospital doctors and nurses, university teachers, lawyers etc. However, the low and high skillful labor market can be enough supply in Hong Kong, but Hong Kong employers need the current high and low both skillful workers who need to work more than 10 to 12 hours or more per working day commonly. It is possible that HK high and low educational labors will be caused unhealthy and lack enough sleep if who still need to work abnormal working hours time in long time. Although, who can rise productivity and efficiency in the short time, but it is possible that who can't rise productivity and inefficiency in the long time. Moreover, it will cause many young or middle or old ages high educational or low educational knowledgeable hardworking workers who will lose many jobs provided and who will be hard to find any jobs in HK labor employment market if HK employers don't choose to pay extra salaries to employ extra full time workers to share current labors' workload in the high and low salary occupations, due to they only choose to increase abnormal additional extra working hours to current workers to achieve to reduce employment expenditure and raise productivity. Hence, it is possible to influence HK social economy grows up slowly, even it's economy can go down seriously in long time.

I shall assume that working wage or salary of every individual labors can not be increased, even can be decreased as well as whose normal working hours can be increased abnormally in generally. This means that the Hong Kong individual worker's income will be decreased and general productivity raising is not affected generally, due to HK employers need current labors to work abnormal extra working hours to attempt to raise productivity daily, but their salary or wage have not increased more. However, HK employers need many workers to accomplish the same amount of work, even who don't like to employ extra labors to assist current workers to achieve long term productivity raising in their companies. These abnormal working hours labors will feel unfair treatment, due to they need to work abnormal working hours, but their salary or wage have not been increased.

In the first scenario of my hypothesis is about that HK labor employment market's general salary or wage has not been increased to the normal proportion of the increased extra abnormal working time(hours). Then, in HK labors market, due to the numbers of labors supply is more than the jobs supply because HK employers don't like to pay more salary or wage expenditure to employ extra labor, but they like to increase extra abnormal working hours to current workers to aim to achieve productivity. So it will cause many HK job seekers with adequate qualifications or with less qualifications who won't find any jobs easily, then the HK the numbers of unemployed people will be increased and their household incomes will decrease to cause many HK household do not like to spend easily. The result will cause a negative effect on HK social private consumption will be decreased and the businessmen' income will be decreased also. So, HK people private consumption decreasing will influence HK economy growth to be slow, even it will cause HK economy declining in the long time.

In the second scenario of my hypothesis is about that Hong Kong workers are fully compensated for the increasing extra abnormal working time(hours) by the abnormal additional working hours calculation. Although, Hong Kong companies' productivity will be raised, but which are not to the extent that it compensates Hong Kong enterprises for their increased wage or salary costs. In fact, Hong Kong enterprises, their costs are passed on to the clients, it causes Hong Kong's economic growth has an impact on international competitiveness to cause economic declining in possible when these enterprises need to raise their products' sale prices to balance their salary or wage cost raising to win their import competitors. Another effect is that Hong Kong individual labor's incomes decrease, which means that Hong Kong private consumption also falls in this scenario to influence HK economic growth seriously. Thus, the HK economic growth problem will be caused, due to these factors lead to a fall in Hong Kong social household private consumption. Consequently, it will cause many HK employers hope to raise Hong Kong productivity and they will raise the total amount of Hong Kong labor actually worked hours will be risen to such as extent as the increasing in normal working time(hours) from 8 or 9 hours per normal working day to 10 or 11 or 12 hours, even more extra abnormal hours per working day to the current labors. But they do not like to spend more salary or wage expenditure to employ full time extra labors, instead of increasing extra abnormal working hours to current labors to achieve productivity of raising, due to the cost will be increased if they choose to employ extra full time labors if they want to raise productivity. However, I feel they will raise productivity in the short term, but they will not raise productivity in the long term when they choose to raise their current labors abnormal working hours per working day.

The assumption will be made regarding to the relationship between the HK labor market's abnormal long time working hours factor and whether it can influence Hong Kong economic growth in long time for this research economic problem. For example, how many hours Hong Kong labor would actually work or how much workers have efficient productivity and efficiency and how much salaries or wages would be affected as a result of the increasing in working time(hours) in Hong Kong employment market.

I shall apply endogenous growth theory to Hong Kong labor market. As this theory indicates that this model also incorporated a new concept of human capital, whose capital is increasing rates of return. Research done in this area has focused on what increases human capital (e.g. education) or technological change (e.g. innovation) to influence HK economic growth. In macro economic environment, it indicates that economic growth means the increase in the market value of the products and services produced by the country's economy over time. It is conventionally measured as the percent rate of increase in real growth domestic product or real GDP. The growth of the ratio of GDP to population (GDP per capital, per capita income). Thus, an increase in growth is caused by more efficient use of inputs is referred to as intensive growth. GDP growth is caused only be increased in such as capital, population or territory is called extensive growth. Thus, in economy growth theory, typically refers growth off potential output, i.e. production is at full employment. However, HK unemployment ratio is still high to compare other developed or developing countries, although the labors supply are enough to HK employment market.

The working time is the period of time that an individual spends at paid occupation labor. Many countries regulate the work week by law, such as minimum daily rest periods, annual holidays and a maximum number of working hours per week. Working time may vary from person to person often depending on location, cultural, lifestyle choice and the profitability of the individual's livelihood.

Generally, most Hong Kong employers need labors work long time working hours abnormally. For example, low educational workers, such as security occupations of labors need to work per working day is twelve hours or more, restaurant waiters and dish cleaners also need to work ten to twelve hours or more per working day, bank counter cashiers or audit firm staffs also need to work over time from 10 to 12 hours or more per working day and who have no extra salaries for over time salaries payment commonly.

Standard working hours or normal working hours refers to the legislation to limit the working hours per day, per week, per month or per year. If an employee needs to work overtime, the employer will need to pay overtime payments to employees as required in the law. Generally speaking, standard working hours countries word wide are around 40 to 44 hours per week (but not everywhere: such as France employers need labors work from 35 hours per week, North Korea employers need labors work up to 112 hours per week). Maximum working hours refers that the employee can't work than the level specified in the maximum working hours law. It seems that Hong Kong many employers had needed labors to work above standard working hours per week to compare to other developed countries, e.g. America, France, England, New Zealand etc. developed countries.

In conclusion, in my viewpoint, HK employers need to provide on job training to current labors to aim to raise their efficiency to productivity in the long time. Because when their labors had been trained to let them to learn how to use special skill to finish their job duties easily, then they will not need to spend much time (additional working hours) to finish their job duties per working day. On the one hand, HK employers need to measure to compare what benefits are in favor of standard working hours to whose employees. The benefits include, such as promoting work life balance and enjoy family life, increasing time for leisure and rest, beneficial to health and employees can have more time to pursue further studies as well as employers do not need to pay higher salaries to longer working hours employees or overtime pay boost income as most HK companies pay time and a half to some employees only. On the other hand, HK employers need to measure to compare what benefits are against standard working hours to employers, such as employing many part time working hours employees to assist normal working hours full time employees rather than needing full time employees work abnormal hours daily, lowering or cancelling year and bonus etc. Moreover, HK employers may also use various measure to offset the increased cost of running businesses, such as lowering average hourly annual compensation. However, when HK employees are forced to work part time jobs, who may need to acquire additional employment to maintain their standard living. Even, HK employers only force employees to work overtime in some situations. Appropriate standard working hours can vary across different industries based on the type of work performed. Such as some HK certain professional positions are difficult to define in terms of appropriate working hours. Issues can arise with employers expecting employees to work extra hours "off the clock" in order to keep costs down. Thus, I believe that HK labors abnormal working hours time issue ought be decreased and HK employers ought employ extra workers assistance to share current labors' workload to help them to raise productivity and efficiency and HK economy will grow fast in the long time. Finally, my research aims to find that the number of hours worked is a more responsive measure of the state of the labor market than employment in HK. Comparing the number of hours worked to indicators of the wider economy shows that it is likely to be demand from HK firms (employers) which is driving the numbers of hours, rather than individual job applicant supply to HK employment market. My analysis also show that the HK appears to have developed a long working hours culture to compare other developed countries, such as America, England, Canada etc. In fact, in the presence of HK firms may even invest to find which are more profitable to able to reduce their every employee's abnormal working hours daily rather than normal number of working hours of their every employee.

Finally, I shall recommend some methods to rise the living standard to low income level households group in any countries. On the income policy, I recommend governments ought implement the progressive tax policy, so the income taxes tend to be progressive to the middle and high income level of households. It aims to achieve the low income level group and the middle and high income level groups whose income level to be balanced. Whereas taxes on payroll and consumption usually are regressive, due to payroll and consumption taxes are more useful than income taxes for increasing revenues taxes on income and payroll are the least conductive to economic growth, so payroll taxes can raise growth of employment in possible. Because the low income level of households have no more effort to spend to buy any expensive products or foods generally, so who can pay less taxes when who spend less. Otherwise, because the middle or high income levels of households have more effort to spend to buy any expensive products or foods generally, so who need pay more taxes when who spend more. It is possible to reduce the level amount of difference of savings between the low income level of households and the middle income level of households. Finally, I conclude that the method of taxes on payroll and consumption usually are regressive and the method of income taxes tend to be progressive to the middle and high income level of households, which are possible to raise the low income level of households of living standard for long term if governments could attempt to achieve these two policies to apply to the low income level group and the middle income level groups both, such as income tax and payroll or consumption tax policies both. It aims to raise the better of standard of life to the low income level household and to assist the low income level household can be upgrade to the middle income level household group in the short time quickly.

Economists claim to be scientists or technicians who study fact, not values, who make scientific studies and predictions to decide why this matter is caused and to find the reasons. Often the public sector economists in USA predict the economic processes and find the facts of the world have not supported the economists‘ models wrongly. However, economists have ethical rules to control their behaviors to be judged any matter and to give the corrective and reasonable decisions to let public to know correctively. Hence, who can't attempt to mislead facts to present to let public to receive the wrongly message to achieve themselves unreasonable benefits and rewards. In fact, economist is similar to lawyer or accountant profession, who need to provide a "service" discipline to give corrective and reasonable judgement and facts and who can not attempt to mislead to publish whose economic research reports to let public to get wrong information frequently. I believe that the scientific of economics of the 20th century fully accepts the ethical separation. Economic theory is seen as a positive science which has to analyze and to explain the mechanisms of economic processes. Ethical valuations should not form part of the economist's research program. Modern economics stresses rational calculation, the base material objections and scientific neutrality on moral issues. I think whose idea is concerned micro economy is based on assumptions of rationally selfish behavior.

Whether what is concerned to current ethical crisis in economics? Economic matters have been debated throughout human history. I feel economic ethical matters which can be concerned in aspects, such as wealth accumulation, lending, business and commerce economic issues, journals or reports or books publishing. Due to any economic matters happen in economic processes which will be recorded in history, then economists will analyze why these issues are caused and find what reasons which cause the economic issue happening is discussed by theology, ethics and politics issues are as view points. So, the moral and ethics is needed to concern to any economists when who need to do any economic research nowadays.

Economy is concerned to human will face limited resources to use or spend, so economy theory indicates to be researched what methods how human chooses to allocate resources to achieve the efficient and effective result. Economy aims to achieve human rationality to control the desire to acquire material products in order to allow better satisfaction of the true human need. Many economists concern for others now directly affects one's own welfare and commitment drives between personal choice and personal welfare and thus undermines modern economics ethic. Individuals frequently display commitment, acting against their own welfare in favor of the group. This element of ethical behavior has been ignored by economists and needs to be brought into the analysis. Although ethical motivation are relevant to economists, but the capabilities approach is more concerned with social achievement. To a large degree, this is a theory of distributive justice that economy and political science and philosophy theories which have more relationship among of these three subjects theories.

Why ethic relates to labor behavior

I shall give some current economists' judgement to indicate how well human are doing according to the capability standard to prove why employers need to concern moral behavior. The capability approaching requires that many means be provided to every person. This is an alternative to social achievement from economics approach, which uses the quantity of commodities available for consumption. The conventional measure of the standard of living (GDP/ head) has been subject to sustained criticism in recent times, one source of the complaints is the capability theorists. This capabilities approach is a new inter-disciplinary social science and there are still many problems with this approach to concern ethical issues of mainstream economics. However, some economists feel that ethical motivations exist and play a role in human's actual behavior. Human well being refers to living a full human life. It measures to show the things that demonstrate a good life being lived. So, human functioning achievements, must be the focus. Possession of a certain quantity of commodities, however, may be necessary in order to achieve human functioning. This provides social success in delivering well being across our society. Moreover, some scientists who also believe the standard of social success may be limited to basic functioning. Alternatively, a rich of human group may be accepted, but social success may be considered for only a small proportion of the population. So, for each theorist, we need to ask these following questions. Does the theorist present an ethical view of motivation? Does the theorist adopt a deep mind of human well being? In the assessment of social success, does the theorist concern human functioning achievements and means to promote functioning achievements?

I shall analyze on individual psychology, household psychology and social achievement three aspects to indicate labor morality and raising productivity and even economic growth has close relationship as below:

In economic view, household means a family which has female control functioning. On the individual and public policy means that support individual achievements. However, in concept analysis, I shall indicate three levels of analysis to economic ethic of human behavior. The lowest level is individual, it is individual psychology, human functioning and ethical motivation. The middle level is household, it is household management, moral education, character formation. The highest level is the city, it is social achievement (Public policy supports equipment needs for individual capability achievement and formative law). So, human's behavioral is an assumption of modern economics. From history viewpoint, our economic conditions are largely agricultural with some mining, manufacturing and commerce, there was limited scope for domestic and international markets; mutual give and take, lending and borrowing between households was widespread. Commonly, these activities are general human economic behavior of reasons to cause these business activities in our society.

Firstly, on individual psychology aspect, human's economy of behavior is in our society, human needs do this economy behavior because human needs have good life and education, the good life required leisure and the good use of leisure time to do leisure activities with friends. Otherwise, leisure required freedom from the duties of earning a living. It was commonly accepted that the good life is required to work to earn, such as labors, traders, professions, farmers etc. service or labor occupations their individual behavior is aim to achieve earning for good life and education. So, who need to spend some time to do economic activities to aim to earn some time for leisure and education.

Secondly, on household management psychology aspect, in general, managing revenues and expenditures is a part of household management. However, household management requires moderation on the desires for food, wine, sex and sleep. So, in labor economy relationship, household seems to be the frame of mind and habits needed for engineering to make sense. In old age, expenditure on subsistence continues, but no one will pay for the labor of the old. Saving for old age, therefore is sensible. However, if one is habituated in youth to lazy, one will find it hand to change later. Nevertheless, these habits are unsustainable in old age, when one can't be labor and generate income. Hence, in labor economy view, moderation is an essential element of good household management. Although, wealth is also important, but more important is the knowledge or skill of household management. However, if one has no leisure and is unable to develop his capabilities (including bodily and non-bodily pleasures to easy to live with). Then, productivity will be reduce and inefficient work, due to the labor is hard to work, who feel himself/herself is such as a machine and who has no much time to rest often. Also the earning of friendship is also important, including certain market relationships in our modern societies. Clearly human's labor economy of behavior of household management in the broad sense is a comprehensive act and part of a way of human life. Hence, an ethical understanding is also needed, such as friendship relationship to complete household management in the middle level of household management between the city level and individual level. On functioning achievement and freedom to individual of labor economy behavior, it includes education, increased physical training etc. economic benefits to our individual in our society. Just as the city is a complex structure, so is human psychology to cause labor economy behavior. Justice in the city is defined as each class (and each individual within the class) doing its own job, justice in the individual is defined as each part of individual doing its own job. Hence, a good city has all of the individuals correctly assigned to the different classes and each individual and each class performs its appropriate job. Similarly, the good individual has each of labor's performing its job appropriately.

In the final social achievement aspect, it concerns micro. As the growth of the healthy city showed up to a certain point, economic development is required in terms of the city's physical size and population. So, modern economic principles are adopted (such as economic development and the division of labor). Nevertheless, our society must be justify to some degree to market relations. Various property rights and exchange justice must be enforced. These principles, however are limited by other ethical principles guiding the laws. Nevertheless, citizens are to be banned from engaging in most occupations. For example, the moral dangers of commercial activities are great. Moreover, market are limited to a specific location and regulated by market regulators. Although, duties are not imposed on foreign trade, prohibitions apply to various unnecessary imports and to exports of necessities. Hence, it will influence labor demand and job supply to influence the country's economic development in any time. To analyze labor economy, we need to know human nature and to establish the functions of human beings. These functions are shared with human beings, e.g. humans need to eat, drink. As a general rule, the passions that drive human to satisfy these needs, but it is of limited amount to supply. So, these factors will influence labor's behavior between action, motivation and character. However, every organization is influenced to economic growth every year by its staff individual behavior, such as its staff individual has passions and emotions disposed toward bad action and decides to act well for other reasons, e.g. the staff feels fear of detection or punishment and then who will act well because of the staff's self control to avoid the firm will dismiss him/her in the firm. It seems the staff's passion, emotion will influence whose behavior to be good or bad to do whose work in whose firm. Hence, the firm needs have economic analysis to decide to dismiss the staff or not dismiss the staff if it discovered whose behavior is not acceptable to its firm and what it will be influenced from whose bad behavior in the short term and long term. If the staff is very important and if who left this firm, this firm will face business failure challenge because it has no any right applicant or another staff who can do this staff's job easily. Hence, in labor economy analysis, the firm needs to judge the benefits are much or the losses are much before which decide to dismiss the staff.

What are ethics? Ethics are a set of values or group of moral principles that are right and good a code or principles of behavior or conduct governing an individual or group. For example, when a engineer needs to do any researching jobs which concern to engineering, who needs to increase whose ability as engineer to responsibly confront moral issues raised by technological activity, not always in short term best interest, and long term into decision making ethics are imprecise, complex, and in a given situation may conflict. Who will have these questions to concern before who does his duties, such as does it pass the benefits /harm test? Whom does it harm? Whom does it benefit? Can these be justified, cost/ benefit analysis risk assessment? Does it treat everyone equally? equitable? If not, can the differences be justified? However, any employer needs to concern whose labor ethics issues, who have four aspects need to be considered, such as: On the first concerning aspect, it is working condition ethics, whether the employer's act is moral right when it respects right relevant to a work environment or employment condition of situation. For example, whether the employer can provide whose employees have rights for life, liberty, pursuit of happiness, human rights and non-human rights, e.g. clean and safe working environment or fair salary and welfare, unreasonable normal working hours. On the second concerning aspect, it is duty ethics, whether the employer acts it is right when it conforms with ethics duties to whose employees, e.g. uphold promise, be fair treatment to job nature and duty, respect personal freedom, duty to protect the weak, duty to comply with employment laws, duty to do job to best of ability. On the third concerning aspect, it is utilitarianism ethic, whether the employer has right action consists in producing good consequences to whose employees, e.g. good intentions, outcomes, honesty, fairness, conscientiousness etc. On the final concerning aspect, it is the situational ethics, which means that depending on the specific circumstance, different rights, duties, values, etc. the right circumstance may be applied to whose labors, e.g. whether the workers work in the dirty and dark factory and who need to work abnormal working hours. It seems that if the working environment is not suitable to the employees to feel to work, it will influence the labors raise to work inefficient and poor performance.

So, employers need to concern their ethics to labor, it include moral development to labor, which are often classified such as, obedience or punishment, marketplace morality, conformity, law and order, social contract, universal human rights and integrity whole environment ethic moral development of issues. However, emotion is one important factor to influence labor's individual performance and productivity and efficiency to any employer. How emotional labor and ethic of care will influence productivity. Employers concern care which ought be more than labor itself. Labor's activity that is fundamentally about maintaining, continuing and repairing the working economic world, so that labor can live in it as well as possible. An ethic of labor care is more than a list of moral principles, the ethic of care labor elements, it includes attentiveness, responsibility, competence and responsiveness. However, employers need to make distinctions between " caring for" and "caring about" to labor ethic. "Caring about" is directed toward less concrete objects/subjects. It is a general form of commitment to employees, when "caring for" focuses on a specific object/ subject and responds to the particular, physical, spiritual, intellectual and emotional needs of labor. Caring labor is too inclusive of all kinds of economic activities. So employers ought not care relations too narrowly, but should include care is given by extended to employees' families, such as domestic workers and workers in hospitals and teachers etc. service labor occupations. So, labor care ethic relates to the work that employers do under the working conditions within which the employers' labor. Also, a labor care ethic is a deeply relational framework involving both labor care activities and practices as well as a habit of labor care mind. So, employers ought presume that dependent is valued, accepted and universal, it necessitates that care labor to every is shared equally and the society policy also needs to be promoted care labor values to let employers to concern this care labor issue. Care ethic means that empathy and responsiveness, among others, coming out of practices and experiences of " doing care".

However, the important aspects of a care ethic that complicates our understanding of the reproduction of alienated labor under capitalism as well as in carrying out care labor, caring for the recipient is an expected part of that work.

In labour ethic view, employers ought attempt to answer this question. Does the expectation of such affective emotions necessitate a different formulation of compensation? In examining the relationship between an ethic of care and the alienation under capitalist relations of production. For example: What does make a "good work" ? Is a good worker someone who cares about whose work? How much should the worker care for the recipient of the labour? What does about the customer service representative who care about assisting someone? or does the retail salesperson care about helping someone look good? or does the carpenter care for the wood with which he is working? Whether the worker may or may not take time, be attentive, responsive and responsible. So, I suggest "caring about" and "caring for" the work and the recipient implies a relational experience with others. Many workers care about the outcome of their labour, whether a final product or service. They take pride in their work, they care about doing a good job, they take care of the people with whom who encounter in the process. In this way, workers make their work meaningful, who attempt to connect to it and to those who are "served" when carrying out the work.

Nowadays, human are encountering of an expended service economy, care and the emotional labour involved in such work. For example, luxury hotel workers are interactive service workers both consented to activity investing in the work, also luxury service is not only about what workers do; it is also about how they do it. Luxury service means that how workers make their jobs meaningful, become invested in them, and construct images of themselves as skilled and autonomous. For example, flight attendants who are the caring and emotional labour that is expected of these workers and it is the caring for the recipient, which allows workers to find meaning, creativity and feel connected to the work itself. I also think that labouring makes "real" something outside of the individual, the commodity as value is imposed external to the thing and to the labour itself. Under conditions of private property, the worker is disconnected from whose own creative powers and the objects of the labour become alien to the worker. So, I think employers ought not take away any labour whose individual's specific life, e.g. For long term abnormal working hours will reduce any labour's leisure and family private time.

However, I think labour can divide two kinds of physical labour and emotional labour. For example, the a factory worker works from whose own body and so who is a physical labour. Otherwise, a flight attendant works from whose own feelings and so who is a emotional labour. However, for the particular features of service -oriented labour, who needs to take "caring for" someone is central, necessarily alter these survival techniques. In care work, it is the consumers/recipients of care who expect that those who do caring work care about the work who do and care for the recipients of their care labour, e.g. hotel employees need to shoe genuine care and concern for guests‘ needs. So, care is the expected and central element of the labour and I think that health attendants and nurses home health carers etc. service workers who need provide more emotional service to whose clients, so who belong to emotional service labour seriously. For example, nursing profession, nurses are thought about as caring, moral creatures who show kindness and comfort to their patients. It is the doctors who are assumed to possess skills and knowledge. How care labour may be negatively affected, such as underpaid, overworked may happen in a situation where the care-giver is compensated unjustly and treated unfairly. Is it possible to argue that if care labour or any labour carried out in the context of a care ethic, the work that is done could be so much better for the whole of society and for the person doing the work and recipients of the work? In an ethic of care that predominates, would we simply value the labour of chid-care workers or home care attendants etc. workers? Would we reflect better compensation, better treatment and better working conditions because our relationship with ourselves and each other are acknowledged and values? Hence, care activities are needed to focus on caring labour, e.g. nurses, personal attendants or home care workers and child care workers. That is, assuming the existence of a care ethic, such questions must be applied to any and all work activities that we do. Does every economic activity contain caring practices, even traditionally non care labour? I think caring about what we do and how we do it, we may help to improve our relations with others, thus reflecting an ethic of care. Does caring labour help to make invisible, reduce its harm to the self and society? It may be true that workers cared for their work, product or service, this would serve the needs of the employers quite well. How do we care for/ about something but against the exploitation produced by capital labour relations? Is it good for society as a whole to care about what you do, care for the work you do, Does the product you make or the service you provide even if it enriches the owner and exploits the worker? What about the office cleaner who cleans the office effectively and efficiently in order to keep whose job that who desperately needs. Should the office cleaner care about doing a good job, care for the faceless people who doesn't know?

A care ethic both encourages this type of work ethic and at the same time, these relations are created and who serve are expected to care for and about the recipients of care, the customer is always right. However, structural inequalities between consumers and workers are normalized in the process. For the nurses and home care workers, the work becomes their own, who become attached to the work, connected to the process and the final outcome, and the work gives meaning to their live. At the same time, when workers don't care about whose work, when they don't care for their charges, or for the service who are offering. Should it, when may the labour be a child care provider neglecting the needs of the child? Or of the overworked social worker dismissing the needs of whose client in order to fill paperwork that who is directed to complete. Hence, I recommend employers need to concern about care is needed such as a practice, value, ethic activity to their labours. The elements of care, its affective emotional and relational qualities help to give meaning to the work for the worker. At the same time, it could be an ethic of care, where individuals view themselves as relational, identifying our connections to others and mutual responsibilities for each other become the necessary conditions for a working class politics.

Labour market equilibrium is a important issue to be concerned in law economy and ethic aspect. Workers prefer to work when the wage is high, and firms prefer to hire when the wage is low generally. Labour market equilibrium "balance out" the conflicting desires of workers and firms and determines the wage and employment observed in the labour market. If labour markets are competitive and if firms and workers are free to enter and leave; the equilibrium allocation of workers to firms is efficient; the sorting of workers and firms are accumulated by trading each other. In fact, labour markets are efficient plays a role by the public policy. Many government programs are often debated whether the particular policy leads to a more efficient allocation of resources or whether the efficiency costs are substantial. Labour market equilibrium occurs when labour supply equals labour demand, generating the competitive wage(w) and employment (E). The wage (w) is the market clearing wage because any other wage level would create either upward or downward pressures on the wage. It would be too many jobs to supply, but the few available workers or too many workers competing for the few available job determined. Due to the competitive wage level is determined in this industry fashion, each firm in the industry hires workers up to the point where the value of marginal product of labour equals the competitive wage. Then, it seems the industry worker's wage level has arrived the maximum labour market wage level. So, employers ought not need to increase whose wage to attract more workers to choose to do whose industry often because it is not reasonable wage level increasing when the labour supply number is enough at the moment. Also the labour market of the industry has implied it's worker demand numbers has arrived the equal level of job supply numbers in the stage. What is caused to happen by worker surplus? When the difference between what the worker receives, that is the competitive wage(w) and the value of the worker's time outside the labour market gives the gains to workers. So, it will cause the excess workers have a value of marginal product that is less than their value of time. In effect, those workers are not being efficiently used by the labour market. So, firms ought to learn how to allocate the right number of persons to different positions that maximizes the total gains and firms ought need to learn how to form trade in the labour market in any efficient allocation way.

Search of labour economy, the central aim is to examine how a work perspective, countries can develop their skills base to increase both the quantity and the productivity of labour employed in the country. Inadequate education and skills of labour development can influence any countries' overall economic development in long term. So, governments need to achieve good policies to solve this issue. Due to skills and education development is central to improve productivity. Because productivity is an important source of improved living standards and growth. Other critical factors include macroeconomic policies maximize opportunities for poor employment growth, an enabling environment is for enterprise development and fundamental investments in education, health and physical to income level households. So, effective skills development systems which is needed to connect education to technical training, technical training to labour market entry and labour market entry to workplace to long life learning to concentrate on providing to low income level households.

Productivity growth can reduce production costs and increase returns on investments. Some of which provide greater income for business owners which some are given higher wages to labours. However, the productivity of individuals may be reflected in employment rates, wage rates, stability of employment, job satisfaction or employability across jobs or industries. The productivity of enterprises, in addition to output per worker may measure in terms of market share and export performance. The benefits to societies from higher individual and enterprise productivity may be evident in increased competitiveness and employment or in a shift of employment from low to higher productivity sector. So, employers can use this method to measure every employee's morality and job behaviour performance to judge whether their job ethic and job attitude whether which can adopt to continue to work in whose organizational environment. If the employer discovered the employee's morality and job behaviour performance and job attitude is not achieved to whose work performance standard, then who can decide to either reduce whose salary or dismiss him/her or not increasing whose salary for long term any decision. So, labour ethic issue is very important to influence economic growth to any countries.

Whether labour ethic has close relationship to economic growth. I feel this issues concerns any stage of the labour life cycle and organization life cycles, it includes the link between the design of economic theory and labour individual morality and job behaviour and performance. In fact, we need to suppose all research questions and labour economy is as mapping to particular stages of an individual's life cycle to labour economy ought be related to the accumulation of human (labour) capital, labour market entry and labour supply choices, behaviour within firms and household decision making. Prior years some researchers had been carrying on observing experiments to the women and men labour work and in whose nature environment for weeks, and then used various treatments, including manipulating the environment in such a way to increase and decrease rest periods. They got result long time working hours and not rest time, it will reduce labours(workers) of productivity. So, it implies the overall productivity and individual productivity will be reduced. Although, the employers have enough workers to work in the natural working environment at the same time, but due to who have no enough rest time to provide to them, then their workers' working performance and efficiency will be fallen. Nowadays, industrialized countries had began to consider how to plan similar welfare reforms, researching the economic reasons and consequences to labour economic issue, such as United States, the United King, Sweden and Germany, it seems economic growth and law ethic has close relationship. However, labour economy includes how to measure labour's emotion to raise productivity, as well as how technological change, education, employment and wages which can assist labour to raise productivity. Due to good labour emotion and labour ethic can raise productivity, then raising productivity can also raise economic growth finally. So, I believe which have close cause and effect relationship.

However, many economists have long been pessimistic that an experimental approach could offer such illustrations of labour ethic and economic growth of cause and effect relationship in their field. Who feel labour bad emotion or bad labour ethic has no any influence to economic growth. In fact, the economic world is extremely complicated, so human needs to have economic laws is set by controlled experiment to measure or judge whether labour ethic and economic growth which has or has no any close relationship. If economists have no such test, economic laws, who can't perform such as the controlled experiments of chemists or biologists very well because who can't easily control other important factors to observe why labour emotion or ethic has reason to influence overall economic growth to any country if they neglect to carry on researching experiment between the relationship of ethic and productivity and economic growth. So I recommend economists need have participants in the natural field experiment to carry on researching to any labour emotion or ethic issue to gather statistic information of population to get prediction more accurately if who want to measure whether labour emotion or ethic and productivity which has close relationship to any country's economic growth for long term.

Why employers need to concern ethic to decide whether outsourcing can raise productivity

Generally, outsourcing can be defined as an organization is entering into a contract with another organization to operate and manage one or more of its business processes. Due to employers face increasing competitive pressure to remain focused, flexible, cost competitive and competent, so outsourcing can access to low cost specialized talent. However, outsourcing means the contracting out of a employer's non core, non efficient, non revenue producing activities to specialists. It is a strategic management tool, such as restructure or contracting out to third party to carry out certain functions efficiently. The most common types of outsourcing are manufacturing outsourcing, information technology outsourcing and business process outsourcing (including processes related to accounting, human resources, benefits, payroll and finance etc. aspects). In fact, employers decide outsourcing reasons which include such as: market pressure to be price competitive, availability of cheap labour elsewhere, abundance of highly talented skilled labour in themselves country, pressure is from investing to cut cost, increase profit and show growth, focusing on core business operations and expanding global presence etc. factors. Many employers begin to concern the ethical and moral implication of outsourcing issue to cause the political and business discussion nowadays. Also, many economists have for-or-against social debates for outsourcing ethic issue. However, outsourcing can bring these benefits to some businesses. For example, if a car can be made more cheaper in China, it should be; if a telephone enquiry can be processed more cheaper in any Asia country, it should be. All such transactions raise real incomes on both sides as resources are advantageously redeployed, with added investment and growth in the exporting country, and lower prices in the importing country.

However, conservative economists argue that the sole mission of a corporation is to maximize profit for the benefits of shareholders. They also contend that in a global economy, outsourcing does not mean net job loss. They argue that more jobs will be created global since the cost labour lowered. The term "global" comes to mind when discussing today's large Corporations. It is hard to say which locally a company belongs to. In fact, outsourcing can also cause disadvantages. Sudden loss of jobs and loss of income can lead to economic depression in smaller regions. As the biggest employer in a those towns/cities closes down factories and start manufacturing in Asia or outsource the manufacturing altogether to a foreign this party. So, the country will raise unemployment rate suddenly when local jobs are outsourced to overseas.

Morality of local employees in favor of outsourcing hiring low wage employees elsewhere is another point of contention of this debate. The (capitalist) economy based on the law of supply and demand. In such economy, allocation or resources, including capital and labour is generally determined by market forces. Therefore, it is reasonable and expectable that companies would seek the best option available to employ their capital and recruit in a global economy. Due to it is assumed that local responsibility has less meaning when the economy and company operate globally. So, it causes any country employers don't concern labour ethic issue after outsourcing influences to its local labour. Nowadays, many employers would agree that the acts of downsizing/ outsourcing for pure financial reasons (i.e. choosing short-term investor gain over employee welfare) are very often morally wrong. However, without clear morally relevant distinction (either in academia or business press) between a company's priority to the shareholder and that to its workers, it is very hard defend that position. This is justified because shareholders have taken a risk in placing their money in the hands of the corporation, and are thereby due compensation. Shareholders can potentially lose something who have placed into the corporation. However, workers have placed something at risk when accepting a job, they lose future potential earnings due to corporate outsourcing. At the very least, the worker has foregone other possible job opportunities. Even more importantly, many workers have invested in their houses, their local communities and in their lifestyle with the expectation of a steady income. When the worker's investment in a corporation is not of the same sort as the shareholder's, it constitutes a risk nevertheless, and so the worker's position is not different to that of the shareholder. However, I believe that evaluating the differences of that risk will depend upon of each individual's relationship with the company and their personal values. For example, CEO pay is a completely separate issue on its own. It is a very popular subject in current academic and business press. Even if it is different subject, it has moral implications in regards to outsourcing. In general, CEO can earn a more percent raise to compare to regular worker's percent raise. In common, companies show the reason of CEO percent raise more is that there is enough causation to conclude that outsourcing contributes to profitability / stock price increase of a company, this the rise in CEO compensation. The ethic issue here is that, if the market rewards a company for improving it is bottom line or for cutting costs why is it ethically wrong for a company to outsource at the expense of local labour force. After all, the reason for an existence of company is to provide value to its shareholders. However, I think CEOs aims to achieve themselves benefits, who may improve their bottom line when hurting workers and communities. The morality of further rewarding CEO's who knowingly undertook layoffs of his employees in favor of outsourcing their work to a third party or move those jobs to a low wage country is very troubling.

In fact, outsourcing raises many concerns for working professional for and communities. It has long held personal and community values, such as , loyalty and commitment to employees. However, as much as economic prosperity global trade can bring, if does bring devastation as well. Availability of cheap products is appreciable, but you need to have a job and a income to consume those products. For many, outsourcing hurts at the heart of their livelihoods.

Also, I argue to against outsourcing is that growing concern of issues of privacy related to outsourcing information creates an ethical and legal issue. The concern is against outsourcing (in specific cases of Accounting, Human Resource and Medical outsourcing) because of the fear of sensitive information's safety and confidentiality. So, employers ought check references and transcripts and perform background checks to minimize the risk of hiring someone who lacks ethic or morality to do whose outsourcing job duties. Moreover, outsourcing firms may indicate that all of their employees are highly educated, trained professionals of the highest honesty. Finally, I recommend employers ought to consider these questions before who decide to outsource, such as: does stockholders welfare out weight that of a company's employees? Is profit maximization ethical? Is it ethical to reward the upper management for cutting cost by eliminating jobs? Should the compensation for upper management with held if the profit is achieved by outsourcing? Is it ethical to reward a management that repeatedly shown disregard to its employees? (increasing workload, constant layoff, choosing the cheapest labour over quality). Is it right for the public to expect a company to keep all its employment locally, (at a higher cost) but at the same time sell products at comparable rate with foreign companies who use cheap labour? Does a company ethically bound a provide maximum occupation in its home country? Does it have a duty to its local community? In case of outsourcing is the employer ethically bound to retrain the employees? So, all these questions are very important concerning outsourcing influence, if every employer can concern these questions, then who can decide whose outsourcing reason is right or wrong more clearly. To conclude, any employer ought need to decide whether outsourcing is the best of one method to raise productivity for long term strategic plan.

How labour morality can reduce poverty in society

In conclusion, I shall use labour morality can assist society to reduce poverty. In labour economy view, a livelihood comprises the capabilities of assets (including both material and social resources) and activities required for a means of living. A livelihood is sustainable when it can cope with and recover from shocks, maintain or enhance its capabilities and asset, when not undermining the natural resource base. It has three elements: livelihood resources, livelihood strategies and institutional processes and organizational structures. So, I think that productivity will raise, even poverty and crime will be also reduced, due to the low income level householder family which can be upgraded to increase whose income level and quality of living standard to the middle income level householder family. When governments can promote the labour morality to which employers to let them to know labour morality and productivity has close relationship.

How to understand the complex and differentiated process through which livelihoods are constructed, governments need to analyse which countries themselves local citizen to let their knowledge, perceptions and interests be heard. There are three insights into poverty. The first is the realization that when economic growth may be essential for poverty reduction, there is not an automatic an automatic relationship between the two since if all depends on the capabilities of the poor to take advantage of expanding economic opportunities. Secondly, there is the realization that poverty as conceived by the poor themselves. It is not just a question of low income, but also includes other factors, such as bad health, illiteracy, lack of social services etc. Finally, it is now often know their situation and need best and must therefore be involved in the design of policies and project intended to better their lot. So, governments and employers need to identify those issues of subjects areas for effective poverty reduction, either at the local level or at the policy level. This is in principle on open-ended process, certain emphasis is given to the introduction of improved technologies as well as social and economic investments to every country's government. The three fundamental attributes to any developing countries or developed countries themselves countries if which plan to raise economic growth and to reduce poverty to upgrade or low income level householders to rise to the middle income level householder family. The three attributes include the possession of human capabilities, such as education, skills, health, psychological orientation; access to tangible and intangible assets and the existence of economic activities. However, a livelihood comprises the capabilities, assets, including both material and social resources and activities required for a means of living. A livelihood is sustainable when it can cope with and recover from stresses and shocks and maintain or enhance its capabilities and assets both now and in the future. To solve poverty problem, it includes not only physical and natural resources, but also every country's social and human capital issues. Every country's government also needs to facilitate an understanding of the causes of poverty by focusing on the variety of factors at different levels that directly or indirectly determine or constrain low income level householder's access to and assets of different kinds. Also every country's government needs to assess the direct and indirect effects on low income level householder's living conditions then, for example one dimensional productivity or income criteria.

Over the various components of a livelihood, the most complex is the portfolio of assets out of which people construct their living. This portfolio includes tangible assets, such as stores, e.g. food stocks, stores of value, such as gold, jewelry, cash saving and resources, e.g. land, water, trees, live stocks farm, equipment as well as intangible assets, such as claims, for example, demands and appeals which can be made be material, moral or other practical support and access, which is the opportunity to practice to use a resource, store or service or to obtain information, material, technology, employment, food or income. Hence, if employers can provide enough capital input to make whose labours feel fairness, satisfactory and reasonable working environment and compensation. I believe that these satisfactory demand of labours who can raise productivity to their employers more easily. In labour economic view, any employers, governments or companies organizational resources inputs can divide four kinds of capital nature. Firstly, the natural capital is natural resources stocks, e.g. soil, water, air, genetic resources etc. and environmental services, e.g. hydrological cycle, pollution sinks, etc. from which resources flows and services useful for livelihoods are derived . Secondly, economic or financial capital is the capital base, e.g. cash , credit/debt, savings and other economic assets, including basic infrastructure and production equipment and technologies which are essential for the pursuit of and livelihood strategy. Thirdly, human capital is the skill, knowledge, ability to labour and good health and physical capability important for the successful pursuit of different livelihood strategies and finally, social capital is the social resources, e.g. networks, social claims, social relations, which people draw when pursuit different livelihood strategies, requiring co-ordinated action. So, any country or employee which has a plan to know how to allocate which resources efficiently, it will raise productivity and economic growth and poverty reducing more easily. So, it seems labour morality can raise productivity which has close relationship to any employer, even labour morality and economic growth which has close relationship to any country. So, any country and any employer which ought not neglect labour morality for long term.

Bibliography

Dimson, Marsh & Staunton, London Business School (2005) In The Global Investment Returns Year Book, ABN Amro.

Fiscal Policy And Long Term Growth, International Monetary Fund, IMF policy papers, Washington, D.C. Available from April, 2015, http://www.imf.org/external/pp/ppindex.aspx.

9 798887 830452

Printed by Libri Plureos GmbH in Hamburg, Germany